Using Water

How You Use and Change Water

DEVELOPED IN COOPERATION
WITH

ORLANDO SCIENCE CENTER
ORLANDO, FLORIDA

Copyright © 1993 by Scholastic Inc. All rights reserved. Published by Scholastic Inc. Printed in the U.S.A.

ISBN 0-590-26144-4

2 3 4 5 6 7 8 9 10   09   99 98 97 96 95 94 93 92

ALL PARTS OF AN ENVIRONMENT ARE INTERRELATED; THEREFORE, CHANGES TO ONE PART AFFECT OTHER PARTS.

Using Water

Water is a natural resource that people use and change in various ways.

Read-Aloud

Using Water

Water is found in various forms in the environment.

Water is a basic necessity of life and a resource for many human activities.

Literature

Most human activities affect water quality.

Literature

Where in the World Is Water?

Water covers most of the earth.

What are different bodies of water called? What bodies of water are closest to where you live?

You need:
Posterboard
Markers or crayons

Locate water.

❶ Draw a map of your area. Show where you live or go to school.

❷ Add any water nearby.

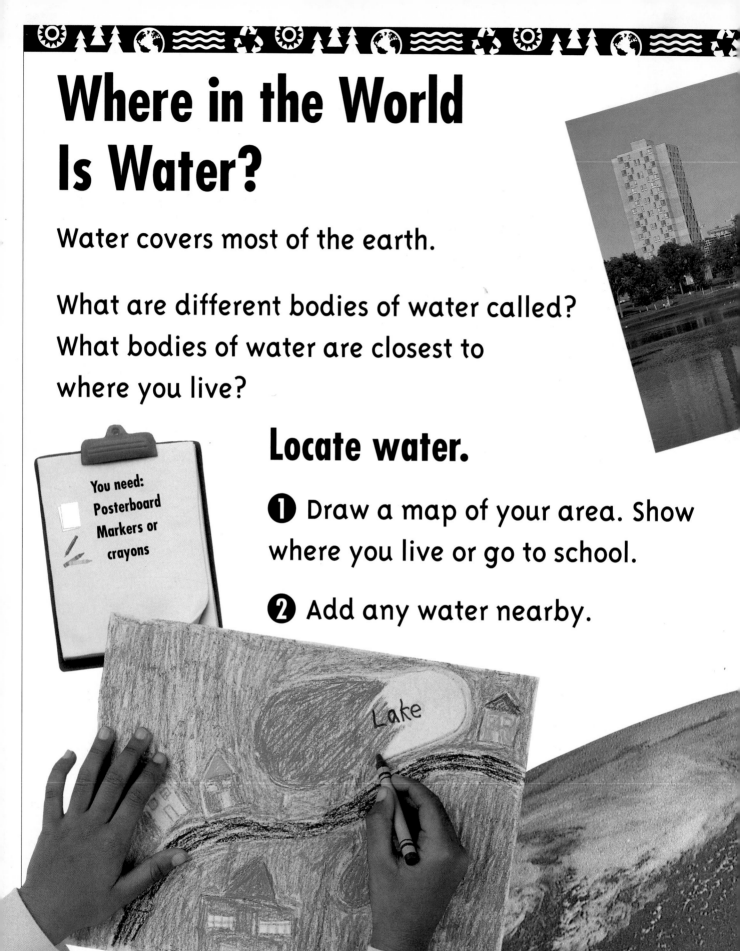

Lake

4

Most of the water in the world is in four great oceans: the Atlantic, the Pacific, the Indian, and the Arctic. Which ocean is closest to you?

THINK!
How is ocean water different from the water you drink?

Where Does Fresh Water Come From?

Most of the water on the earth is salty ocean water.
But people need fresh water.
How does the sun help change salt water to fresh water?

You need:
Black paper
Small clear cup
Tape
Warm water
Spoonful of salt
Wax paper
Large clear cup
Rubber band

Make a solar still.

❶ Wrap and tape black paper around the small cup.

❷ Add water and salt. Stir. Taste the water. Set the cup on wax paper in the sun.

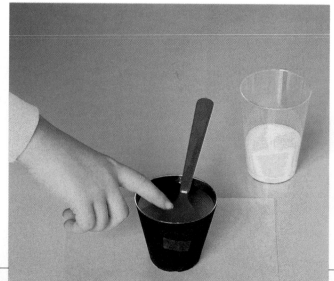

3 Place the large cup over the small one. Pull up the wax paper and hold it with a rubber band.

4 Wait three hours, and wipe your finger inside the large cup. Taste it. What happened?

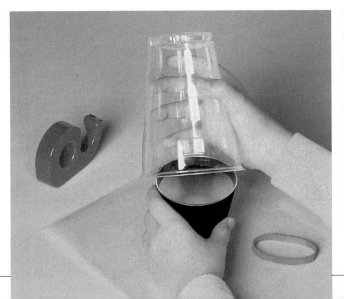

THINK!
What would happen if you used white paper instead of black?

How Does Fresh Water Move?

The water in your solar still evaporated, or changed to a gas. This gas was water vapor.

As water vapor rises, it cools and collects into drops. Raindrops are too heavy for air to hold, so they fall.

How else does water move? What happens when lots of water drops get together?

Make a pile of water.

❶ Predict how many drops of water will fit on a penny.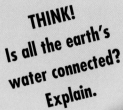

❷ Squeeze one drop of water onto the penny. What happens?

❸ Now carefully squeeze one drop at a time. How many more drops will fit?

THINK!
Is all the earth's water connected? Explain.

Where Does Fresh Water Go?

Water falls and flows from one place to another. Where does it go? How does it change the land as it flows?

Make a river.

❶ Put wet sand in the pan, and place some pebbles around. Raise one end of the pan with blocks.

❷ Shake a wet sponge over the raised end and over the middle. What happens?

❸ Now slowly pour a cup of water on the the raised end. Where does the water go?

You need:
Pan
Wet sand
Pebbles
Blocks
Cup
Water
Sponge

Through streams and lakes and rivers and swamps, water makes its long journey to the ocean.

THINK!
Can water travel under the ground? Explain.

How Do Living Things Use Water?

In and along all of water's paths, you'll find living things. Why?

How do plants use water?

How do animals use water?

How Do You Use Water?

How many ways do you use water? How much water do you drink in one day? Which foods that you eat have water in them?

Keep a water diary.

❶ Make a column that lists all the ways you use water. Make one column for each day of the week.

❷ Keep track of how many times you use water in each way every day.

THINK!
Do you have
water inside you?
Explain.

How Do People Collect Water?

Farms, factories, and towns need a lot of water. People have to collect and move water to where they need it.

Some people dig wells in the earth to reach underground water.

A reservoir can collect large amounts of water. People make a reservoir by building a dam to block the natural flow of a river.

THINK!
Where is the water stored for your town?

How Do People Move Water?

People need to move water from their wells or reservoirs to where they can use it. How do they do it?

You need:
- Pan
- Newspaper
- Water
- Blue food dye
- Clear cup
- Tubing

Build a water tunnel.

1 Pour a few cups of blue water into a pan. Fill a cup halfway with water.

2 Fill the tube with water, and place a finger over each end. Put one end in the pan and the other in the cup. Keep both ends in water.

3 Remove your fingers from the ends, but keep the tube in water. What happens?

THINK!
How does water get to people in your area?

What Happens to Water After People Use It?

Water moves through pipes to and from the places where people use it. In some areas, each house has its own system for getting rid of dirty water.

Build a septic system.

① Label one large cup Septic Tank. Poke holes around the bottom. Put it in a pan and cover the holes with sand.

You need:
Sand
Pan
Water
Dirt
Red food dye
Soap
Cups
Tubing
Spoon

❷ Label the other large cup House. Poke a small hole close to the bottom, and put in the tube. Raise the House so the tube goes down to the Septic Tank.

❸ In three small cups, put soap, red food dye, and dirt. Add water to each. Pour each kind of dirty water through the septic system. What happens?

THINK!
What would happen to plants growing in that sand?

How Does Water Get Polluted?

Water is often polluted after people use it. Pollution is anything that can spoil clean water or air or land. What pollution do you see in this picture?

Where does pollution go once it gets into water?

You need:
Your water map
Markers or crayons

Draw a pollution route.

1 On the water map you made, choose a place for pollution to start.

2 Draw what makes the pollution and trace the route it takes.

3 Draw some living things it passes. How can pollution affect them?

THINK!
How can pollution get into a well if nobody throws anything in?

What Does Water Pollution Do?

When dirty water empties into lakes, rivers, and soil, whole water systems can become polluted.

What can polluted water do to living things?

You need:
- Pan
- Water
- Eyedropper
- Cooking oil
- Feather
- Cotton balls
- String
- Paper towels

Make an oil spill model.

❶ Fill a pan with water and add a few drops of oil. What happens? ✏️

❷ Blow air on your oil spill. What happens now? ✏️

❸ Dip the feather in the water. What do you see? How can you clean the feather? Try it. ✏️

❹ How can you clean up the oil on the water? Try your materials. ✏️

THINK! What can people do to clean up oil spills?

What Can People Do About Water Pollution?

Pollution affects all living things, so people look for ways to stop or get rid of it. Can filters get rid of water pollution?

Test water filters.

You need:
Water
Soap
Sand
Two pans
Three cups
Cooking oil
Paper filter
Sharp pencil
Food dye

❶ Fill a cup with water. Add oil, soap, and food dye. Stir, and set this cup aside.

❷ Punch tiny holes in the bottoms of two clean cups. Push a paper filter into one cup, and put that cup in a pan.

3 Put sand in the other cup with holes, and put that cup in the second pan.

4 Pour half the polluted water into the sand and half into the paper filter. What happens?

THINK!
How could people stop pollution from happening?

How Can People Save Water?

Pollution ruins millions of gallons of water. Every day, everywhere, people also waste water. Often they don't even know how much they waste. How fast does water get away down the drain?

Be a water detective.

❶ Predict how long it takes to fill a milk carton with water.

❷ Turn on the faucet and see how long it really takes.

How many cartons of water go down the drain if the water runs while you brush your teeth?

You need:
Running water
Milk carton
Clock

Who's wasting water here?
Who's saving it?

THINK!
How can you use
old water again?

How Important Is Water?

Every year there are more and more people on the earth, but there's always just the same amount of water. Every living thing uses water and then gives it back to the water cycle.

From ocean to sky to mountain to river, around and around the same water goes, again and again, year after year.

You need:
Your water diary
Posterboard
Markers or crayons

Create a conservation poster.

❶ Draw some ways animals and plants use water. Use your water diary to help you.

❷ Show the ways people waste or pollute water. Show how you can save and protect water.

❸ Hang your posters in the classroom or in the school hallway.

Conservation: Conservation is saving natural resources like water as much as possible.

Dam: A dam is a wall that blocks the flow of water. People build dams to store water and to control the flow of the water.

Evaporation: Evaporation happens when water changes from a liquid into a gas. This gas, called water vapor, makes clouds.

Filter: Filters separate smaller objects from larger ones. A filter lets small pieces pass through, but stops larger pieces.

Fresh water: Most lakes, streams, and rivers are filled with fresh water. Fresh water falls to earth as rain. It has much less salt in it than ocean water does.

Pollution: Pollution is waste or leftover material that can spoil clean air, water, land, or other natural resources.